A GARLAND OF IRISH VERSE

A GARLAND OF IRISH VERSE

With Illustrations by
W. Lee Hankey

Edited by Gwynn Hayes

Gramercy Books
New York • Avenel

Compilation and Introduction
copyright © 1993 by Outlet Book Company, Inc.
All rights reserved

This 1993 edition is published by Gramercy Books
distributed by Outlet Book Company, Inc.
a Random House Company
40 Engelhard Avenue
Avenel, New Jersey 07001

Designed by Melissa Ring

Random House
New York • Toronto • London • Sydney • Auckland

Printed and bound in the United States of America

Library of Congress Cataloging-in-Publication Data
A Garland of Irish verse.
p. cm.
ISBN 0-517-08487-2
1. English poetry—Celtic authors. 2. English poetry—Irish
authors. 3. Ireland—Poetry. I. Gramercy Books (Firm)
PR8496.G37 1993   93-22848
821.008'09415—dc20   CIP

8 7 6 5 4 3 2 1

CONTENTS

INTRODUCTION

The poetic genius of the Irish stretches in a long, unbroken chain over hundreds of years. From the earliest period of Irish history the names of famous bards are known. Indeed, in ancient Gaelic Ireland the poet was a powerful official. Modern Irish poetry stems from the poetic revival that began at the end of the seventeenth century. The poets were men of the people and they wrote of the people's suffering and sorrow, as well as of their dreams and their joys.

A Garland of Irish Verse is a sampling of Ireland's poetic riches. The early poems were translated from the Gaelic by such outstanding Celtic scholars as Whitley Stokes and George Sigerson, by such fine poets as Samuel Ferguson, Padraic Pearse, and Edward Walsh, and by Charlotte Brooke, who in the eighteenth century gave momentum to the Irish Celtic Revival.

Many of the poems in this collection were written in the English language by men and women of Irish birth. Some of these Anglo-Irish poets were educated and spent most of their early, formative years in Ireland.

Jonathan Swift, three of whose charming poems are included here, was the first great figure of Anglo-Irish letters. Oliver Goldsmith, represented with his moving poem "The Deserted Village," was born and educated in Ireland, yet he is seldom considered an Irish writer so fully has his work been absorbed into the stream of English literature. Among the other Anglo-Irish poets included in this anthology is Thomas Moore, whose lyrical poetry strongly influenced English poets and who made the world aware of Irish music. There are poems by

Gerald Griffin, considered one of the most brilliant of Anglo-Irish novelists; Katharine Tynan Hinkson, who was inspired by the Pre-Raphaelites; Francis Ledwidge, who was killed during World War I while fighting with the British forces in France; Padraic Pearse, one of the three martyred leaders of the Irish Rebellion of 1916; and, of course, William Butler Yeats, the great star in the poetic firmament who found the universal voice to sing of his own country.

This is an exciting collection of lusty, vigorous, singing verse, of exquisite paeans to nature and passionate poems of love. It is a selection that attests to Ireland's great literary heritage.

GWYNN HAYES

New York
1993

PRAYER TO ST. PATRICK

We invoke holy Patrick, Ireland's chief apostle.
Glorious is his wondrous name, a flame that baptized heathen;
He warred against hard-hearted wizards.
He thrust down the proud with the help of our Lord of fair
    heaven.
He purified Ireland's meadowlands, a mighty birth.
We pray to Patrick chief apostle; his judgment hath delivered
    us in Doom from the malevolence of dark devils.
God be with us, together with the prayer of Patrick, chief
    apostle.

NININE

*Translated by Whitley Stokes
and John Strachan*

EIRE

When Eire first rose from the dark-swelling flood,
God blessed the green island, and saw it was good;
The emerald of Europe, it sparkled and shone,
In the ring of the world, the most precious stone.
In her sun, in her soil, in her station thrice blest,
With her back towards Britain, her face to the west,
Eire stands proudly insular, on her steep shore,
And strikes her high harp 'mid the ocean's deep roar.

But when its soft tones seem to mourn and to weep,
A dark chain of silence is thrown o'er the deep;
At the thought of the past the tears gush from her eyes,
And the pulse of her heart makes her white bosom rise.
O! sons of green Eire, lament o'er the time
When religion was war, and our country a crime;
When man in God's image inverted His plan,
And molded his God in the image of man.

When the interest of state wrought the general woe,
The stranger a friend, and the native a foe;
While the mother rejoiced o'er her children oppressed,
And clasped the invader more close to her breast;
When, with Pale for the body and Pale for the soul,
Church and State joined in compact to conquer the whole;
And, as Shannon was stained with Milesian blood,
Eyed each other askance and pronounced it was good.

By the groans that ascend from your forefathers' grave,
For their country thus left to the brute and the slave,
Drive the demon of Bigotry home to his den,
And where Britain made brutes now let Eire make men.
Let my sons like the leaves of the shamrock unite,
A partition of sects from one footstalk of right,
Give each his full share of the earth and the sky,
Nor fatten the slave where the serpent would die.

Alas! for poor Eire, that some are still seen
Who would dye the grass red from their hatred to Green;
Yet, O! when you're up and they're down, let them live,
Then yield them that mercy which they would not give.
Arm of Eire, be strong! but be gentle as brave!
And, uplifted to strike, be still ready to save!
Let no feeling of vengeance presume to defile
The cause of, or men of, the Emerald Isle.

The cause it is good, and the men they are true,
And the Green shall outlive both the Orange and Blue!
And the triumphs of Eire her daughters shall share,
With the full swelling chest, and the fair flowing hair.
Their bosom heaves high for the worthy and brave,
But no coward shall rest on that soft-swelling wave;
Men of Eire! awake, and make haste to be blest,
Rise—Arch of the Ocean, and Queen of the West!

WILLIAM DRENNAN

AH! WHAT WOES ARE MINE

Ah! what woes are mine to bear,
   Life's fair morn with clouds o'ercasting!
Doomed the victim of despair!
   Youth's gay bloom, pale sorrow blasting!

Sad the bird that sings alone,
   Flies to wilds, unseen to languish,
Pours, unheard, the ceaseless moan,
   And wastes on desert air its anguish!

Mine, O hapless bird! thy fate—
   The plundered nest—the lonely sorrow!
The lost—loved—harmonious mate!
   The wailing night—the cheerless morrow!

O thou dear hoard of treasured love!
   Though these fond arms should ne'er possess thee,
Still—still my heart its faith shall prove,
   And its last sighs shall breathe to bless thee!

EDMOND O'RYAN
Translated by Charlotte Brooke

THE DAWNING OF THE DAY

At early dawn I once had been
　Where Lene's blue waters flow,
When summer bid the groves be green,
　The lamp of light to glow.
As on by bower, and town, and tower,
　And widespread fields I stray,
I met a maid in the greenwood shade
　At the dawning of the day.

Her feet and beauteous head were bare,
　No mantle fair she wore;
But down her waist fell golden hair,
　That swept the tall grass o'er.
With milking pail she sought the vale,
　And bright her charms' display;
Outshining far the morning star
　At the dawning of the day.

Beside me sat that maid divine
　Where grassy banks outspread.
"Oh, let me call thee ever mine,
　Dear maid," I sportive said.
"False man, for shame, why bring me blame?"
　She cried, and burst away—
The sun's first light pursued her flight
　At the dawning of the day.

AUTHOR UNKNOWN
Translated by Edward Walsh

LOVE'S DESPAIR

I am desolate,
Bereft by bitter fate;
No cure beneath the skies can save me,
   No cure on sea or strand,
   Nor in any human hand—
But hers, this paining wound who gave me.

   I know not night from day,
   Nor thrush from cuckoo gray,
Nor cloud from the sun that shines above thee—
   Nor freezing cold from heat,
   Nor friend—if friend I meet;
I but know—heart's love!—I love thee.

   Love that my life began,
   Love that will close life's span,
Love that grows ever by love-giving;
   Love from the first to last,
   Love till all life be passed,
Love that loves on after living!

   This love I gave to thee,
   For pain love has given me,
Love that can fail or falter never—
   But, spite of earth above,
   Guards thee, my flower of love,
Thou marvel-maid of life, for ever.

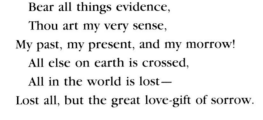

Bear all things evidence,
Thou art my very sense,
My past, my present, and my morrow!
All else on earth is crossed,
All in the world is lost—
Lost all, but the great love-gift of sorrow.

My life not life, but death:
My voice not voice—a breath;
No sleep, no quiet—thinking ever
On thy fair phantom face,
Queen eyes and royal grace,
Lost loveliness that leaves me never.

I pray thee grant but this:
From thy dear mouth one kiss,
That the pang of death-despair pass over:
Or bid make ready nigh
The place where I shall lie,
For aye, thy leal and silent lover.

DIARMAD O'CURNAIN
Translated by George Sigerson

IDEAL

Naked I saw thee,
O beauty of beauty!
And I blinded my eyes
For fear I should flinch.

I heard thy music,
O sweetness of sweetness!
And I shut my ears
For fear I should fail.

I kissed thy lips
O sweetness of sweetness!
And I hardened my heart
For fear of my ruin.

I blinded my eyes
And my ears I shut,
I hardened my heart,
And my love I quenched.

I turned my back
On the dream I had shaped,
And to this road before me
My face I turned.

I set my face
To the road here before me,
To the work that I see,
To the death that I shall meet.

PADRAIC PEARSE
Translated by Thomas MacDonagh

HOW HAPPY THE LITTLE BIRDS

How happy the little birds
That rise up on high
And make music together
On a single bough!
Not so with me
And my hundred thousand loves:
Far apart on us
Rises every day.

Whiter she than the lily,
Than beauty more fair,
Sweeter voiced than the violin,
More lightsome than the sun;
Yet beyond all that
Her nobleness, her mind,—
And O God Who art in Heaven,
Relieve my pain!

AUTHOR UNKNOWN
Translated by Padraic Pearse

APPLES

Come buy my fine wares,
Plums, apples, and pears.
A hundred a penny,
In conscience too many:
Come, will you have any?
My children are seven,
I wish them in heaven;
My husband a sot,
With his pipe and his pot,
Not a farthing will gain them,
And I must maintain them.

ONIONS

Come, follow me by the smell,
Here are delicate onions to sell;
I promise to use you well.
They make the blood warmer,
You'll feed like a farmer;
For this is every cook's opinion,
No savory dish without an onion;
But, lest your kissing should be spoiled,
Your onions must be thoroughly boiled:
Or else you may spare
Your mistress a share,
The secret will never be known:
She cannot discover
The breath of her lover,
But think it as sweet as her own.

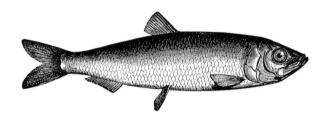

HERRINGS

Be not sparing,
Leave off swearing.
Buy my herring
Fresh from Malahide,
Better never was tried.
Come, eat them with pure fresh butter and mustard,
Their bellies are soft, and as white as a custard.
Come, sixpence a dozen, to get me some bread,
Or, like my own herrings, I soon shall be dead.

JONATHAN SWIFT

THE DESERTED VILLAGE

Sweet Auburn! loveliest village of the plain;
Where health and plenty cheered the laboring swain,
Where smiling spring its earliest visit paid,
And parting summer's lingering blooms delayed:
Dear lovely bowers of innocence and ease,
Seats of my youth, when every sport could please,
How often have I loitered o'er thy green,
Where humble happiness endeared each scene!
How often have I paused on every charm,
The sheltered cot, the cultivated farm,
The never-failing brook, the busy mill,
The decent church that topped the neighboring hill,
The hawthorn bush, with seats beneath the shade,
For talking age and whispering lovers made!
How often have I blest the coming day,
When toil remitting lent its turn to play,
And all the village train, from labor free,
Led up their sports beneath the spreading tree,
While many a pastime circled in the shade,
The young contending as the old surveyed;
And many a gambol frolicked o'er the ground,
And sleights of art and feats of strength went round.
And still, as each repeated pleasure tired,
Succeeding sports the mirthful band inspired;
The dancing pair that simply sought renown,
By holding out to tire each other down;
The swain mistrustless of his smutted face,
While secret laughter tittered round the place;
The bashful virgin's side-long looks of love,
The matron's glance that would those looks reprove:
These were thy charms, sweet village! sports like these,
With sweet succession, taught even toil to please:

These round thy bowers their cheerful influence shed:
These were thy charms—but all these charms are fled.
    Sweet smiling village, loveliest of the lawn,
Thy sports are fled, and all thy charms withdrawn:
Amidst thy bowers the tyrant's hand is seen,
And desolation saddens all thy green:
One only master grasps the whole domain,
And half a tillage stints thy smiling plain.
No more thy glassy brook reflects the day,
But, choked with sedges, works its weedy way;
Along thy glades, a solitary guest,
The hollow sounding bittern guards its nest;
Amidst thy desert walks the lapwing flies,
And tires their echoes with unvaried cries;
Sunk are thy bowers in shapeless ruin all,
And the long grass o'er-tops the moldering wall;
And trembling, shrinking from the spoiler's hand,
Far, far away thy children leave the land.

    Ill fares the land, to hastening ills a prey,
Where wealth accumulates, and men decay:
Princes and lords may flourish, or may fade;
A breath can make them, as a breath has made;
But a bold peasantry, their country's pride,
When once destroyed, can never be supplied.

    A time there was, ere England's griefs began,
When every rood of ground maintained its man;
For him light labor spread her wholesome store,
Just gave what life required, but gave no more:
His best companions, innocence and health;
And his best riches, ignorance of wealth.

    But times are altered; trade's unfeeling train
Usurp the land and dispossess the swain;

Along the lawn, where scattered hamlets rose,
Unwieldy wealth and cumbrous pomp repose,
And every want to opulence allied,
And every pang that folly pays to pride.
Those gentle hours that plenty bade to bloom,
Those calm desires that asked but little room,
Those healthful sports that graced the peaceful scene,
Lived in each look, and brightened all the green;
These, far departing, seek a kinder shore,
And rural mirth and manners are no more.

Sweet Auburn! parent of the blissful hour,
Thy glades forlorn confess the tyrant's power.
Here, as I take my solitary rounds
Amidst thy tangling walks and ruined grounds,
And, many a year elapsed, return to view
Where once the cottage stood, the hawthorn grew,
Remembrance wakes with all her busy train,
Swells at my breast, and turns the past to pain,

In all my wanderings round this world of care,
In all my grief—and God has given my share—
I still had hopes, my latest hours to crown,
Amidst these humble bowers to lay me down;
To husband out life's taper at the close,
And keep the flame from wasting by repose:
I still had hopes, for pride attends us still,
Amidst the swains to show my book-learned skill,
Around my fire an evening group to draw,
And tell of all I felt, and all I saw;
And, as an hare whom hounds and horns pursue,
Pants to the place from whence at first she flew,
I still had hopes, my long vexations past,
Here to return—and die at home at last.
O' blest retirement, friend to life's decline,

Retreats from care, that never must be mine,
How happy he who crowns in shades like these,
A youth of labor with an age of ease;
Who quits a world where strong temptations try,
And, since 'tis hard to combat, learns to fly!
For him no wretches, born to work and weep,
Explore the mine, or tempt the dangerous deep;
No surly porter stands in guilty state,
To spurn the imploring famine from the gate;
But on he moves to meet his latter end,
Angels around befriending Virtue's friend;
Bends to the grave with unperceived decay,
While resignation gently slopes the way;
And, all his prospects brightening to the last,
His heaven commences ere the world be past!

Sweet was the sound, when oft at evening's close
Up yonder hill the village murmur rose.
There, as I passed with careless steps and slow,
The mingling notes came softened from below;
The swain responsive as the milk-maid sung,
The sober herd that lowed to meet their young,
The noisy geese that gabbled o'er the pool,
The playful children just let loose from school,
The watch-dog's voice that bayed the whispering wind,
And the loud laugh that spoke the vacant mind;—
These all in sweet confusion sought the shade,
And filled each pause the nightingale had made.
But now the sounds of population fail,
No cheerful murmurs fluctuate in the gale,
No busy steps the grass-grown foot-way tread,
For all the bloomy flush of life is fled.
All but yon widowed, solitary thing,
That feebly bends beside the plashy spring:
She, wretched matron, forced in age, for bread,
To strip the brook with mantling cresses spread,

To pick her wintry faggot from the thorn,
To seek her nightly shed, and weep 'til morn;
She only left of all the harmless train,
The sad historian of the pensive plain.

    Near yonder copse, where once the garden smiled,
And still where many a garden flower grows wild;
There, where a few torn shrubs the place disclose,
The village preacher's modest mansion rose.
A man he was to all the country dear,
And passing rich with forty pounds a year;
Remote from towns he ran his godly race,
Nor e'er had changed, nor wished to change his place;
Unpracticed he to fawn, or seek for power,
By doctrines fashioned to the varying hour;
Far other aims his heart had learned to prize,
More skilled to raise the wretched than to rise.
His house was known to all the vagrant train;
He chid their wanderings but relieved their pain:
The long-remembered beggar was his guest,
Whose beard descending swept his aged breast;
The ruined spendthrift, now no longer proud,
Claimed kindred there, and had his claims allowed;
The broken soldier, kindly bade to stay,
Sat by the fire, and talked the night away,
Wept o'er his wounds or, tales of sorrow done,
Shouldered his crutch and showed how fields were won.
Pleased with his guests, the good man learned to glow,
And quite forgot their vices in their woe;
Careless their merits or their faults to scan
His pity gave ere charity began.

    Thus to relieve the wretched was his pride,
And e'en his failings leaned to Virtue's side;
But in his duty prompt at every call,
He watched and wept, he prayed and felt for all;

And, as a bird each fond endearment tries
To tempt its new-fledged offspring to the skies,
He tried each art, reproved each dull delay,
Allured to brighter worlds, and led the way.

    Beside the bed where parting life was laid,
And sorrow, guilt, and pain by turns dismayed,
The reverend champion stood. At his control
Despair and anguish fled the struggling soul;
Comfort came down the trembling wretch to raise,
And his last faltering accents whispered praise.

    At church, with meek and unaffected grace,
His looks adorned the venerable place;
Truth from his lips prevailed with double sway,
And fools, who came to scoff, remained to pray.
The service past, around the pious man,
With steady zeal, each honest rustic ran;
Even children followed with endearing wile,
And plucked his gown to share the good man's smile.
His ready smile a parent's warmth exprest;
Their welfare pleased him, and their cares distrest:
To them his heart, his love, his griefs were given,
But all his serious thoughts had rest in heaven.
As some tall cliff that lifts its awful form,
Swells from the vale, and midway leaves the storm,
Though round its breast the rolling clouds are spread,
Eternal sunshine settles on its head.

    Beside yon straggling fence that skirts the way,
With blossomed furze unprofitably gay,
There, in his noisy mansion, skilled to rule,
The village master taught his little school.
A man severe he was, and stern to view;
I knew him well, and every truant knew;
Well had the boding tremblers learned to trace

The day's disasters in his morning face;
Full well they laughed with counterfeited glee
At all his jokes, for many a joke had he;
Full well the busy whisper circling round
Conveyed the dismal tidings when he frowned.
Yet he was kind, or, if severe in aught,
The love he bore to learning was in fault;
The village all declared how much he knew:
'Twas certain he could write, and cipher too;
Lands he could measure, terms and tides presage,
And even the story ran that he could gauge;
In arguing, too, the parson owned his skill,
For, even though vanquished, he could argue still;
While words of learned length and thundering sound
Amazed the gazing rustics ranged around;
And still they gazed, and still the wonder grew,
That one small head could carry all he knew.

But past is all his fame. The very spot
Where many a time he triumphed, is forgot.
Near yonder thorn, that lifts its head on high,
Where once the sign-post caught the passing eye,
Low lies that house where nut-brown draughts inspired,
Where graybeard mirth and smiling toil retired,
Where village statesmen talked with looks profound,
And news much older than their ale went round.
Imagination fondly stoops to trace
The parlor splendors of that festive place:
The white-washed wall, the nicely sanded floor,
The varnished clock that clicked behind the door;
The chest contrived a double debt to pay,
A bed by night, a chest of drawers by day;
The pictures placed for ornament and use,
The twelve good rules, the royal game of goose;
The hearth, except when winter chilled the day,
With aspen boughs and flowers and fennel gay;

While broken teacups, wisely kept for show,
Ranged o'er the chimney, glistened in a row.

   Vain transitory splendors! could not all
Reprieve the tottering mansion from its fall?
Obscure it sinks, nor shall it more impart
An hour's importance to the poor man's heart.
Thither no more the peasant shall repair
To sweet oblivion of his daily care;
No more the farmer's news, the barber's tale,
No more the woodman's ballad shall prevail;
No more the smith his dusky brow shall clear,
Relax his ponderous strength, and lean to hear;
The host himself no longer shall be found
Careful to see the mantling bliss go round;
Nor the coy maid, half willing to be prest,
Shall kiss the cup to pass it to the rest.

   Yes! let the rich deride, the proud disdain,
These simple blessings of the lowly train;
To me more dear, congenial to my heart,
One native charm, than all the gloss of art.
Spontaneous joys, where Nature has its play,
The soul adopts, and owns their first born sway;
Lightly they frolic o'er the vacant mind,
Unenvied, unmolested, unconfined.
But the long pomp, the midnight masquerade,
With all the freaks of wanton wealth arrayed—
In these, ere triflers half their wish obtain,
The toiling pleasure sickens into pain;
And, even while fashion's brightest arts decoy,
The heart distrusting asks if this be joy.

   Ye friends to truth, ye statesmen, who survey
The rich man's joy increase, the poor's decay,

'Tis yours to judge, how wide the limits stand
Between a splendid and an happy land.
Proud swells the tide with loads of freighted ore,
And shouting Folly hails them from her shore;
Hoards even beyond the miser's wish abound,
And rich men flock from all the world around.
Yet count our gains! This wealth is but a name
That leaves our useful products still the same.
Not so the loss. The man of wealth and pride
Takes up a space that many poor supplied;
Space for his lake, his park's extended bounds,
Space for his horses, equipage, and hounds:
The robe that wraps his limbs in silken sloth
Has robbed the neighboring fields of half their growth;
His seat, where solitary sports are seen,
Indignant spurns the cottage from the green:
Around the world each needful product flies,
For all the luxuries the world supplies;
While thus the land adorned for pleasure all
In barren splendor feebly waits the fall.
As some fair female unadorned and plain,
Secure to please while youth confirms her reign,
Slights every borrowed charm that dress supplies,
Nor shares with art the triumph of her eyes;
But when those charms are past, for charms are frail,
When time advances, and when lovers fail,
She then shines forth, solicitous to bless,
In all the glaring impotence of dress.
Thus fares the land by luxury betrayed:
In nature's simplest charms at first arrayed,
But verging to decline, its splendors rise,
Its vistas strike, its palaces surprise;
While, scourged by famine from the smiling land
The mournful peasant leads his humble band,
And while he sinks, without one arm to save,
The country blooms—a garden and a grave.

Where then, ah! where shall poverty reside,
To 'scape the pressure of contiguous pride?
If to some common's fenceless limits strayed,
He drives his flock to pick the scanty blade,
Those fenceless fields the sons of wealth divide,
And even the bare-worn common is denied.

If to the city sped—what waits him there?
To see profusion that he must not share;
To see ten thousand baneful arts combined
To pamper luxury, and thin mankind;
To see those joys the sons of pleasure know
Extorted from his fellow-creature's woe.
Here while the courtier glitters in brocade,
There the pale artist plies the sickly trade;
Here while the proud their long-drawn pomps display,
There the black gibbet glooms beside the way.
The dome where Pleasure holds her midnight reign,
Here, richly decked, admits the gorgeous train:
Tumultuous grandeur crowds the blazing square,
The rattling chariots clash, the torches glare.
Sure scenes like these no troubles e'er annoy!
Sure these denote one universal joy!
Are these thy serious thoughts?—Ah, turn thine eyes
Where the poor houseless shivering female lies.
She once, perhaps, in village plenty blest,
Has wept at tales of innocence distrest;
Her modest looks the cottage might adorn,
Sweet as the primrose peeps beneath the thorn;
Now lost to all; her friends, her virtue fled,
Near her betrayer's door she lays her head,
And, pinched with cold, and shrinking from the shower,
With heavy heart deplores that luckless hour,
When idly first, ambitious of the town,
She left her wheel and robes of country brown.

Do thine, sweet Auburn, thine, the loveliest train,
Do thy fair tribes participate her pain?
Even now, perhaps, by cold and hunger led,
At proud men's doors they ask a little bread!
Ah, no! To distant climes, a dreary scene,
Where half the convex world intrudes between,
Through torrid tracts with fainting steps they go,
Where wild Altama murmurs to their woe.
Far different there from all that charmed before
The various terrors of that horrid shore;
Those blazing suns that dart a downward ray,
And fiercely shed intolerable day;
Those matted woods, where birds forget to sing,
But silent bats in drowsy clusters cling;
Those poisonous fields with rank luxuriance crowned.
Where the dark scorpion gathers death around;
Where at each step the stranger fears to wake
The rattling terrors of the vengeful snake;
Where crouching tigers wait their hapless prey,
And savage men more murderous still than they;
While oft in whirls the mad tornado flies,
Mingling the ravaged landscape with the skies.
Far different these from every former scene,
The cooling brook, the grassy vested green,
The breezy covert of the warbling grove,
That only sheltered thefts of harmless love.

Good Heaven! what sorrows gloomed that parting day,
That called them from their native walks away:
When the poor exiles, every pleasure past,
Hung round the bowers, and fondly looked their last,
And took a long farewell, and wished in vain
For seats like these beyond the western main,
And shuddering still to face the distant deep,
Returned and wept, and still returned to weep.

The good old sire, the first prepared to go
To new found worlds, and wept for others' woe;
But for himself, in conscious virtue brave,
He only wished for worlds beyond the grave.
His lovely daughter, lovelier in her tears,
The fond companion of his helpless years,
Silent went next, neglectful of her charms,
And left a lover's for a father's arms.
With louder plaints the mother spoke her woes,
And blest the cot where every pleasure rose,
And kist her thoughtless babes with many a tear
And claspt them close, in sorrow doubly dear,
Whilst her fond husband strove to lend relief,
In all the silent manliness of grief

    O Luxury! thou curst by Heaven's decree,
How ill exchanged are things like these for thee!
How do thy potions, with insidious joy,
Diffuse their pleasure only to destroy!
Kingdoms by thee, to sickly greatness grown,
Boast of a florid vigor not their own.
At every draught more large and large they grow,
A bloated mass of rank, unwieldy woe;
Till sapped their strength, and every part unsound,
Down, down, they sink, and spread a ruin round.

    Even now the devastation is begun,
And half the business of destruction done;
Even now, methinks, as pondering here I stand,
I see the rural virtues leave the land.
Down where yon anchoring vessel spreads the sail
That idly waiting flaps with every gale,
Downward they move, a melancholy band,
Pass from the shore, and darken all the strand.
Contented toil, and hospitable care,

And kind connubial tenderness, are there;
And piety with wishes placed above,
And steady loyalty, and faithful love.
And thou, sweet Poetry, thou loveliest maid,
Still first to fly where sensual joys invade;
Unfit in these degenerate times of shame
To catch the heart, or strike for honest fame;
Dear charming nymph, neglected and decried,
My shame in crowds, my solitary pride;
Thou source of all my bliss, and all my woe,
That found'st me poor at first, and keep'st me so;
Thou guide by which the nobler arts excel,
Thou nurse of every virtue fare thee well!
Farewell, and oh! where'er thy voice be tried,
On Torno's cliff or Pambamarca's side,
Whether where equinoctial fervors glow,
Or winter wraps the polar world in snow,
Still let thy voice, prevailing over time,
Redress the rigors of the inclement clime;
Aid slighted truth with thy persuasive strain;
Teach erring man to spurn the rage of gain:
Teach him, that states of native strength possest,
Though very poor, may still be very blest;
That trade's proud empire hastes to swift decay,
As ocean sweeps the labored mole away;
While self-dependent power can time defy,
As rocks resist the billows and the sky.

OLIVER GOLDSMITH

THE TIME I'VE LOST IN WOOING

The time I've lost in wooing,
In watching and pursuing
   The light that lies
   In woman's eyes,
Has been my heart's undoing.
Though wisdom oft has taught me
I scorn the lore that bought me,
   My only books
   Were woman's looks,
And folly's all they've taught me.

Her smile when beauty granted,
I hung with gaze enchanted,
   Like him, the sprite,
   Whom maids by night
Oft meet in glen that's haunted.
Like him, too, beauty won me,
But while her eyes were on me,
   If once their ray
   Was turned away,
Oh! winds could not outrun me.

Are those follies going!
And is my proud heart growing
   Too cold or wise
   For brilliant eyes
Again to set it glowing?
No—vain, alas! the endeavor
From bonds so sweet to sever;—
   Poor wisdom's chance
   Against a glance
Is now as weak as ever!

THOMAS MOORE

OH BLAME NOT THE BARD

Oh blame not the bard if he flies to the bowers
   Where pleasure lies carelessly smiling at fame;
He was born for much more, and in happier hours
   His soul might have burned with a holier flame.
The string that now languishes loose o'er the lyre,
   Might have bent a bright bow to the warrior's dart,
And the lip which now breathes but the song of desire,
   Might have poured the full tide of a patriot's heart!

But, alas for his country!—her pride is gone by,
   And that spirit is broken which never would bend.
O'er the ruin her children in secret must sigh,
   For 'tis treason to love her, and death to defend.
Unprized are her sons, till they've learned to betray;
   Undistinguished they live, if they shame not their sires;
And the torch that would light them through dignity's way
   Must be caught from the pile where their country expires!

Then blame not the bard, if, in pleasure's soft dream,
   He should try to forget what he never can heal;
Oh! give but a hope—let a vista but gleam
   Through the gloom of his country, and mark how he'll feel!
That instant his heart at her shrine would lay down
   Every passion it nursed, every bliss it adored,
While the myrtle, now idly entwined with his crown,
   Like the wreath of Harmodius, should cover his sword.

But though glory be gone, and though hope fade away,
   Thy name, loved Erin! shall live in his songs;
Not even in the hour when his heart is most gay
   Will he lose the remembrance of thee and thy wrongs!
The stranger shall hear thy lament on his plains;
   The sigh of thy harp shall be sent o'er the deep,
Till thy masters themselves, as they rivet thy chains,
   Shall pause at the song of their captive and weep!

THOMAS MOORE

THE MINSTREL BOY

The minstrel boy to the war is gone,
   In the ranks of death you'll find him,
His father's sword he has girded on,
   And his wild harp slung behind him.
"Land of song!" said the warrior bard,
   "Though all the world betrays thee,
One sword, at least, thy rights shall guard,
   One faithful harp shall praise thee!"

The minstrel fell!—but the foeman's chain
   Could not bring his proud soul under;
The harp he loved ne'er spoke again,
   For he tore its chords asunder;
And said, "No chains shall sully thee,
   Thou soul of love and bravery!
Thy songs were made for the pure and free,
   They shall never sound in slavery!"

THOMAS MOORE

BELIEVE ME, IF ALL THOSE ENDEARING
YOUNG CHARMS

Believe me, if all those endearing young charms,
   Which I gaze on so fondly today,
Were to change by tomorrow, and fleet in my arms,
   Like fairy gifts fading away!
Thou wouldst still be adored, as this moment thou art,
   Let thy loveliness fade as it will,
And around the dear ruin each wish of my heart
   Would entwine itself verdantly still.

It is not while beauty and youth are thine own,
   And thy cheeks unprofaned by a tear,
That the fervor and faith of a soul may be known,
   To which time will but make thee more dear!
Oh the heart that has truly loved never forgets,
   But as truly loves on to the close,
As the sunflower turns to her god when he sets
   The same look which she turned when he rose!

THOMAS MOORE

THE LAST ROSE OF SUMMER

'Tis the last rose of summer,
  Left blooming alone;
All her lovely companions
  Are faded and gone;
No flower of her kindred,
  No rose bud is nigh
To reflect back her blushes,
  Or give sigh for sigh!

I'll not leave thee, thou lone one!
  To pine on the stem;
Since the lovely are sleeping,
  Go, sleep thou with them;
Thus kindly I scatter
  Thy leaves o'er the bed,
Where thy mates of the garden
  Lie scentless and dead.

So soon may I follow,
  When friendships decay,
And from love's shining circle
  Thy gems drop away!
When true hearts lie withered,
  And fond ones are flown,
Oh! who would inhabit
  This bleak world alone?

THOMAS MOORE

PEACE TO THE SLUMBERERS!

Peace to the slumberers!
  They lie on the battle plain
With no shroud to cover them
  The dew and the summer rain
Are all that weep over them.
            Peace to the slumberers!

Vain was their bravery!
  The fallen oak lies where it lay
Across the wintry river;
  But brave hearts, once swept away
Are gone, alas! forever.
            Vain was their bravery!

Woe to the conqueror!
  Our limbs shall lie as cold as theirs
Of whom his sword bereft us,
  Ere we forget the deep arrears
Of vengeance they have left us!
            Woe to the conqueror!

THOMAS MOORE

LOVE IS A HUNTER BOY

Love is a hunter boy,
   Who makes young hearts his prey
And, in his nets of joy,
   Ensnares them night and day.
In vain concealed they lie—
   Love tracks them everywhere;
In vain aloft they fly—
   Love shoots them flying there.

But 'tis his joy most sweet,
   At early dawn to trace
The print of Beauty's feet,
   And give the trembler chase.
And if, through virgin snow,
   He tracks her footsteps fair,
How sweet for Love to know
   None went before him there.

THOMAS MOORE

THE HARP THAT ONCE THROUGH TARA'S HALLS

The harp that once through Tara's halls
   The soul of music shed,
Now hangs as mute on Tara's walls
   As if that soul were fled.
So sleeps the pride of former days,
   So glory's thrill is o'er,
And hearts that once beat high for praise,
   Now feel that pulse no morel

No more to chiefs and ladies bright
   The harp of Tara swells;
The chord alone that breaks at night,
   Its tale of ruin tells.
Thus Freedom now so seldom wakes,
   The only throb she gives
Is when some heart indignant breaks,
   To show that still she lives.

THOMAS MOORE

IF I MIGHT CHOOSE

If I might choose where my tired limbs shall lie
When my task here is done, the oak's green crest
   Shall rise above my grave—a little mound,
Raised in some cheerful village cemetery.
   And I could wish, that, with unceasing sound,
A lonely mountain rill was murmuring by—
   In music—through the long soft twilight hours.
And let the hand of her, whom I love best,
   Plant round the bright green grave those fragrant flowers
In whose deep bells the wild bee loves to rest;
   And should the robin from some neighboring tree
Pour his enchanted song—oh! softly tread,
For sure, if aught of earth can soothe the dead,
   He still must love that pensive melody!

JOHN ANSTER

WHAT WILL YOU DO, LOVE?

"What will you do, love, when I am going,
With white sail flowing,
  The seas beyond?
What will you do, love, when waves divide us,
And friends may chide us
  For being fond?"
"Though waves divide us, and friends be chiding,
In faith abiding,
  I'll still be true!
And I'll pray for thee on the stormy ocean,
In deep devotion—
  That's what I'll do!"

"What would you do, love, if distant tidings
Thy fond confidings
    Should undermine?
And I, abiding 'neath sultry skies,
Should think other eyes
    Were as bright as thine?"
"Oh, name it not!—though guilt and shame
Were on thy name,
    I'd still be true:
But that heart of thine—should another share it—
I could not bear it!
    What would I do?"

"What would you do, love, when home returning,
With hopes high-burning,
    With wealth for you,
If my bark, which bounded o'er foreign foam,
Should be lost near home—
    Ah! what would you do?"
"So thou wert spared—I'd bless the morrow
In want and sorrow,
    That left me you;
And I'd welcome thee from the wasting billow,
This heart thy pillow—
    That's what I'd do!"

SAMUEL LOVER

THE ANGELS WHISPER

A baby was sleeping,
Its mother was weeping,
For her husband was far on the wild raging sea;
And the tempest was swelling
Round the fisherman's dwelling,
And she cried, "Dermot, darling, oh! come back to me."

Her beads while she number'd,
The baby still slumber'd,
And smiled in her face as she bended her knee;
"Oh blest be that warning,
My child's sleep adorning,
For I know that the angels are whispering with thee.

"And while they are keeping
Bright watch o'er thy sleeping,
Oh, pray to them softly, my baby, with me
And say thou wouldst rather
They'd watch o'er thy father!
For I know that the angels are whispering with thee."

The dawn of the morning
Saw Dermot returning,
And the wife wept with joy her babe's father to see;
And closely caressing
Her child, with a blessing,
Said, "I knew that the angels were whispering with thee."

SAMUEL LOVER

LAST NIGHT

I sat with one I love last night,
She sang to me an olden strain;
In former times it woke delight,
    Last night—but pain.

Last night we saw the stars arise,
But clouds soon dimmed the ether blue;
And when we sought each other's eyes
    Tears dimmed them too!

We paced along our favorite walk,
But paced in silence broken-hearted:
Of old we used to smile and talk;
    Last night—we parted.

GEORGE DARLEY

SLEEP THAT LIKE THE COUCHÉD DOVE

Sleep, that like the couchéd dove,
　　Broods o'er the weary eye,
Dreams that with soft heavings move
　　The heart of memory—
Labor's guerdon, golden rest,
Wrap thee in its downy vest;
Fall like comfort on thy brain,
And sing the hush-song to thy pain!

Far from thee be startling fears,
　　And dreams the guilty dream;
No banshee scare thy drowsy ears
　　With her ill-omened scream.
But tones of fairy minstrelsy
Float like the ghosts of sound o'er thee,
Soft as the chapel's distant bell,
And lull thee to a sweet farewell.

Ye, for whom the ashy hearth
　　The fearful housewife clears—
Ye, whose tiny sounds of mirth
　　The nighted carman hears—
Ye, whose pigmy hammers make
The wonderers of the cottage wake—
Noiseless be your airy flight,
Silent as the still moonlight.

Silent go and harmless come,
　　Fairies of the stream—
Ye, who love the winter gloom,
　　Or the gay moonbeam—
Hither bring your drowsy store,
Gathered from the bright lusmore,
Shake o'er temples—soft and deep—
The comfort of the poor man's sleep.

GERALD GRIFFIN

LINES ADDRESSED TO A SEAGULL

White bird of the tempest! oh, beautiful thing,
With the bosom of snow, and the motionless wing;
Now sweeping the billow, now floating on high,
Now bathing thy plumes in the light of the sky;
Now poising o'er ocean thy delicate form,
Now breasting the surge with thy bosom so warm;
Now darting aloft, with a heavenly scorn,
Now shooting along, like a ray of the morn;
Now lost in the folds of the cloud-curtained dome,
Now floating abroad like a flake of the foam;
Now silently poised o'er the war of the main,
Like the spirit of charity brooding o'er pain;
Now gliding with pinion, all silently furled,
Like an angel descending to comfort the world!
Thou seem'st to my spirit—as upward I gaze,
And see thee, now clothed in mellowest rays,
Now lost in the storm-driven vapors that fly
Like hosts that are routed across the broad sky—
Like a pure spirit, true to its virtue and faith
'Mid the tempests of nature, of passion, and death!

Rise! beautiful emblem of purity! rise
On the sweet winds of heaven, to thine own brilliant skies,
Still higher! still higher! till lost to our sight,
Thou hidest thy wings in a mantle of light;
And I think how a pure spirit gazing on thee
Must long for the moment—the joyous and free—
When the soul, disembodied from nature, shall spring,
Unfetterèd, at once to her Maker and King;
When the bright day of service and suffering past,
Shapes fairer than thine shall shine round her at last,
While the standard of battle triumphantly furled,
She smiles like a victor, serene on the world!

GERALD GRIFFIN

THE SHANDON BELLS

Sabbata pango
Funera plango
Solemnia clango

Inscription on an old bell

With deep affection
And recollection
I often think of
   Those Shandon bells,
Whose sounds so wild would,
In the days of childhood,
Fling round my cradle
   Their magic spells.
On this I ponder
Where'er I wander,
And thus grow fonder,
   Sweet Cork, of thee,
With thy bells of Shandon,
That sound so grand on
The pleasant waters
   Of the river Lee.

I've heard bells chiming
Full many a clime in,
Tolling sublime in
   Cathedral shrine,
While at a glib rate
Brass tongues would vibrate—
But all their music
   Spoke naught like thine;
For memory dwelling
On each proud swelling
Of the belfry knelling
   Its bold notes free,
Made the bells of Shandon
Sound far more grand on
The pleasant waters
   Of the river Lee.

I've heard bells tolling
Old "Adrian's Mole" in
Their thunder rolling
   From the Vatican,
And cymbals glorious
Swinging uproarious
In the gorgeous turrets
   Of Notre Dame;
But thy sounds were sweeter
Than the dome of Peter
Flings o'er the Tiber
   Pealing solemnly;
Oh! the bells of Shandon
Sound far more grand on
The pleasant waters
   Of the river Lee.

There's a bell in Moscow,
While a tower and kiosk o!
In Saint Sophia
   The Turkman gets,
And loud in air
Calls men to prayer
From the tapering summit
   Of tall minarets.
Such empty phantom
I freely grant them;
But there is an anthem
   More dear to me,
'Tis the bells of Shandon
That sound so grand on
The pleasant waters
   Of the river Lee.

FRANCIS S. MAHONEY

DEIRDRE'S LAMENT FOR THE
SONS OF USNACH

The lions of the hill are gone,
And I am left alone—alone—
Dig the grave both wide and deep,
For I am sick, and fain would sleep!

The falcons of the wood are flown,
And I am left alone—alone—
Dig the grave both deep and wide,
And let us slumber side by side.

The dragons of the rock are sleeping,
Sleep that wakes not for our weeping—
Dig the grave, and make it ready,
Lay me on my true love's body.

Lay their spears and bucklers bright
By the warriors' sides aright;
Many a day the three before me
On their linkèd bucklers bore me.

Lay upon the low grave floor,
'Neath each head, the blue claymore;
Many a time the noble three
Reddened these blue blades for me.

Lay the collars, as is meet,
Of their grayhounds at their feet;
Many a time for me have they
Brought the tall red deer to bay.

In the falcon's jesses throw,
Hook and arrow, line and bow;
Never again, by stream or plain,
Shall the gentle woodsmen go.

Sweet companions, ye were ever—
Harsh to me, your sister, never;
Woods and wilds, and misty valleys,
Were with you as good 's a palace.

O, to hear my true love singing,
Sweet as sound of trumpets ringing;
Like the sway of ocean swelling
Rolled his deep voice round our dwelling.

O! to hear the echoes pealing
Round our green and fairy sheeling,
When the three, with soaring chorus,
Passed the silent skylark o'er us.

Echo now, sleep, morn and even—
Lark alone enchant the heaven!
Ardan's lips are scant of breath,
Neesa's tongue is cold in death.

Stag, exult on glen and mountain—
Salmon, leap from loch to fountain—
Heron, in the free air warm ye—
Usnach's sons no more will harm ye!

Erin's stay no more you are,
Rulers of the ridge of war;
Never more 't will be your fate
To keep the beam of battle straight!

Woe is me! by fraud and wrong,
Traitors false and tyrants strong,
Fell Clan Usnach, bought and sold,
For Barach's feast and Conor's gold!

Woe to Eman, roof and wall!
Woe to Red Branch, hearth and hall!
Tenfold woe and black dishonor
To the foul and false Clan Conor!

Dig the grave both wide and deep,
Sick I am, and fain would sleep!
Dig the grave and make it ready,
Lay me on my true love's body.

SAMUEL FERGUSON

THE MEMORY OF THE DEAD (1798)

Who fears to speak of Ninety-Eight?
　　Who blushes at the name?
When cowards mock the patriot's fate,
　　Who hangs his head for shame?
He's all a knave, or half a slave,
　　Who slights his country thus;
But a true man, like you, man,
　　Will fill your glass with us.

We drink the memory of the brave,
　　The faithful and the few:
Some lie far off beyond the wave,
　　Some sleep in Ireland, too;
All, all are gone; but still lives on
　　The fame of those who died;
All true men, like you, men,
　　Remember them with pride.

Some on the shores of distant lands
　　Their weary hearts have laid,
And by the stranger's heedless hands
　　Their lonely graves were made;
But, though their clay be far away
　　Beyond the Atlantic foam,
In true men, like you, men,
　　Their spirit's still at home.

The dust of some is Irish earth,
  Among their own they rest,
And the same land that gave them birth
  Has caught them to her breast;
And we will pray that from their clay
  Full many a race may start
Of true men, like you, men,
  To act as brave a part.

They rose in dark and evil days
  To right their native land;
They kindled here a living blaze
  That nothing shall withstand.
Alas! that Might can vanquish Right—
  They fell and passed away;
But true men, like you, men,
  Are plenty here today.

Then here's their memory—may it be
  For us a guiding light,
To cheer our strife for liberty,
  And teach us to unite—
Through good and ill, be Ireland's still,
  Though sad as theirs your fate,
And true men be you, men,
  Like those of Ninety-Eight.

JOHN KELLS INGRAM

THE CELTS

Long, long ago, beyond the misty space
    Of twice a thousand years,
In Erin old there dwelt a mighty race,
    Taller than Roman spears;
Like oaks and towers they had a giant grace,
    Were fleet as deers,
With wind and waves they made their 'biding place,
    These western shepherd seers.

Their Ocean-God was Manannan MacLir,
    Whose angry lips,
In their white foam, full often would inter
    Whole fleets of ships;
Cromah their Day-God, and their Thunderer
    Made morning and eclipse;
Bride was their Queen of Song, and unto her
    They prayed with fire-touched lips.

Great were their deeds, their passions and their sports;
    With clay and stone
They piled on strath and shore those mystic forts,
    Not yet o'erthrown;
On cairn-crowned hills they held their council-courts;
    While youths alone,
With giant dogs, explored the elk resorts,
    And brought them down.

Of these was Finn, the father of the Bard
    Whose ancient song
Over the clamor of all change is heard,
    Sweet-voiced and strong.
Finn once o'ertook Grania, the golden-haired.
    The fleet and young;
From her the lovely, and from him the feared,
    The primal poet sprung.

Ossian! two thousand years of mist and change
    Surround thy name—
Thy Fenian heroes now no longer range
    The hills of fame.
The very names of Finn and Gaul sound strange—
    Yet thine the same—
By miscalled lake and desecrated grange—
    Remains, and shall remain!

The Druid's altar and the Druid's creed
    We scarce can trace,
There is not left an undisputed deed
    Of all your race,
Save your majestic song, which hath their speed,
    And strength and grace;
In that sole song, they live and love, and bleed—
    It bears them on through space.

O, inspired giant! shall we e'er behold,
    In our own time,
One fit to speak your spirit on the wold,
    Or seize your rhyme?
One pupil of the past, as mighty-souled
    As in the prime,
Were the fond, fair, and beautiful, and bold—
    They of your song sublime!

THOMAS D'ARCY MCGEE

THE LEPRAHAUN

In a shady nook one moonlit night,
   A leprahaun I spied
In scarlet coat and cap of green,
   A cruiskeen by his side.
'Twas tick, tack, tick, his hammer went,
   Upon a weeny shoe,
And I laughed to think of a purse of gold,
   But the fairy was laughing too.

With tip-toe step and beating heart,
   Quite softly I drew nigh.
There was mischief in his merry face,
   A twinkle in his eye;
He hammered and sang with tiny voice,
   And sipped the mountain dew;
Oh! I laughed to think he was caught at last,
   But the fairy was laughing, too.

As quick as thought I grasped the elf,
   "Your fairy purse," I cried,
"My purse?" said he, "'tis in her hand,
   That lady by your side."
I turned to look, the elf was off,
   And what was I to do?
Oh! I laughed to think what a fool I'd been,
   And, the fairy was laughing too.

ROBERT DWYER JOYCE

EARLY THOUGHTS

Oh gather the thoughts of your early years,
   Gather them as they flow,
For all unmarked in those thoughts appears
   The path where you soon must go.

Full many a dream will wither away,
   And springtide hues are brief,
But the lines are there of the autumn day,
   Like the skeleton in the leaf.

The husbandman knows not the worth of his seed
   Until the flower be sprung,
And only in age can we rightly read
   The thoughts that we thought when young.

WILLIAM EDWARD HARTPOLE LECKY

AFTER DEATH

Shall mine eyes behold thy glory, O my country?
　　Shall mine eyes behold thy glory?
Or shall the darkness close around them, ere the sunblaze
　　Break at last upon thy story?

When the nations ope for thee their queenly circle,
　　As a sweet new sister hail thee,
Shall these lips be sealed in callous death and silence,
　　That have known but to bewail thee?

Shall the ear be deaf that only loved thy praises,
　　When all men their tribute bring thee?
Shall the mouth be clay that sang thee in thy squalor,
　　When all poets' mouths shall sing thee?

Ah! the harpings and the salvos and the shoutings
　　Of thy exiled sons returning!
I should hear, tho' dead and moldered, and the grave-damps
　　Should not chill my bosom's burning.

Ah! the tramp of feet victorious! I should hear them
　　'Mid the shamrocks and the mosses,
And my heart should toss within the shroud and quiver,
　　As a captive dreamer tosses.

I should turn and rend the cere-clothes round me,
　　Giant sinews I should borrow—
Crying, "O, my brothers, I have also loved her
　　In her loneliness and sorrow!

"Let me join with you the jubilant procession;
　　Let me chant with you her story;
Then contented I shall go back to the shamrocks.
　　Now mine eyes have seen her glory!"

FANNY PARNELL

REQUIESCAT

Tread lightly, she is near
   Under the snow,
Speak gently, she can hear
   The daisies grow.

All her bright golden hair
   Tarnished with rust,
She that was young and fair
   Fallen to dust.

Lily-like, white as snow,
   She hardly knew
She was a woman, so
   Sweetly she grew.

Coffin-board, heavy stone,
   Lie on her breast,
I vex my heart alone,
   She is at rest.

Peace, Peace, she cannot hear
   Lyre or sonnet,
All my life's buried here,
   Heap earth upon it.

OSCAR WILDE

THE WIND THAT SHAKES THE BARLEY

There's music in my heart all day,
  I hear it late and early,
It comes from fields are far away,
  The wind that shakes the barley.
      Ochone!

Above the uplands drenched with dew,
  The sky hangs soft and pearly,
An emerald world is listening to
  The wind that shakes the barley.
      Ochone!

Above the bluest mountain crest
  The lark is singing rarely,
It rocks the singer into rest,
  The wind that shakes the barley.
      Ochone!

Oh, still through summers and through springs
  It calls me late and early.
Come home, come home, come home, it sings,
  The wind that shakes the barley.
      Ochone!

KATHARINE TYNAN HINKSON

AEDH TELLS OF THE ROSE IN HIS HEART

All things uncomely and broken, all things
    worn out and old,
The cry of a child by the roadway, the creak of
    a lumbering cart,
The heavy steps of the ploughman, splashing
    the wintry mold,
Are wronging your image that blossoms a rose
    in the deeps of my heart.

The wrong of unshapely things is a wrong too
    great to be told;
I hunger to build them anew and sit on a green
    knoll apart,
With the earth and the sky and the water,
    remade, like a casket of gold
For my dreams of your image that blossoms a
    rose in the deeps of my heart.

W. B. YEATS

THE MADNESS OF KING GOLL

I sat on cushioned otter skin:
My word was law from Ith to Emen,
And shook at Invar Amargin
The hearts of the world-troubling seamen,
And drove tumult and war away
From girl and boy and man and beast;
The fields grew fatter day by day,
The wild fowl of the air increased;
And every ancient Ollave said,
While he bent down his fading head,
"He drives away the Northern cold."
They will not hush, the leaves a-flutter round
*   me, the beech leaves old.*

I sat and mused and drank sweet wine;
A herdsman came from inland valleys,
Crying, the pirates drove his swine
To fill their dark-beaked hollow galleys.
I called my battle-breaking men,
And my loud brazen battle-cars
From rolling vale and rivery glen;
And under the blinking of the stars
Fell on the pirates by the deep,
And hurled them in the gulph of sleep:
These hands won many a torque of gold.
They will not hush, the leaves a-flutter round
*   me, the beech leaves old.*

But slowly, as I shouting slew
And trampled in the bubbling mire,
In my most secret spirit grew
A whirling and a wandering fire:
I stood: keen stars above me shone,
Around me shone keen eyes of men:
I laughed aloud and hurried on
By rocky shore and rushy fen;
I laughed because birds fluttered by,
And starlight gleamed, and clouds flew high,
And rushes waved and waters rolled.
*They will not hush, the leaves a-flutter round
        me, the beech leaves old.*

And now I wander in the woods
When summer gluts the golden bees,
Or in autumnal solitudes
Arise the leopard-colored trees;
Or when along the wintry strands
The cormorants shiver on their rocks;
I wander on, and wave my hands,
And sing, and shake my heavy locks.
The gray wolf knows me; by one ear
I lead along the woodland deer;
The hares run by me growing bold.
*They will not hush, the leaves a-flutter round
        me, the beech leaves old.*

I came upon a little town,
That slumbered in the harvest moon,
And passed a-tiptoe up and down,
Murmuring, to a fitful tune,
How I have followed, night and day,
A tramping of tremendous feet,
And saw where this old tympan lay,
Deserted on a doorway seat,
And bore it to the woods with me;
Of some unhuman misery
Our married voices wildly trolled.
They will not hush, the leaves a-flutter round
me, the beech leaves old.

I sang how, when day's toil is done,
Orchil shakes out her long dark hair
That hides away the dying sun
And sheds faint odors through the air:
When my hand passed from wire to wire
It quenched, with sound like falling dew,
The whirling and the wandering fire;
But lift a mournful ulalu,
For the kind wires are torn and still,
And I must wander wood and hill
Through summer's heat and winter's cold.
They will not hush, the leaves a-flutter round
me, the beech leaves old.

W. B. YEATS

INTO THE TWILIGHT

Out-worn heart, in a time outworn,
Come clear of the nets of wrong and right;
Laugh heart again in the gray twilight,
Sigh, heart, again in the dew of the morn.

Your mother Erie is always young,
Dew ever shining and twilight gray;
Though hope fall from you and love decay,
Burning in fires of a slanderous tongue.

Come, heart, where hill is heaped upon hill:
For there the mystical brotherhood
Of sun and moon and hollow and wood
And river and stream work out their will;

And God stands winding His lonely horn,
And time and the world are ever in flight;
And love is less kind than the gray twilight,
And hope is less dear than the dew of the morn.

W. B. YEATS

THE LAKE ISLE OF INNISFREE

I will arise and go now, and go to Innisfree,
　And a small cabin build there, of clay and wattles made;
Nine bean rows will I have there, a hive for the honey bee,
　And live alone in the bee-loud glade.

And I shall have some peace there, for peace comes dropping slow,
　Dropping from the veils of the morning to where the cricket sings;
There midnight's all a glimmer, and noon a purple glow,
　And evening full of the linnet's wings.

I will arise and go now, for always night and day
　I hear lake water lapping with low sounds by the shore;
While I stand on the roadway, or on the pavements gray,
　I hear it in the deep heart's core.

W. B. YEATS

TO THE ROSE UPON THE ROOD
OF TIME

Red Rose, proud Rose, sad Rose of all my days!
Come near me, while I sing the ancient ways:
Cuhoollin battling with the bitter tide;
The Druid, gray, wood-nurtured, quiet-eyed,
Who cast round Fergus dreams, and ruin untold;
And thine own sadness, whereof stars, grown old
In dancing silver sandalled on the sea,
Sing in their high and lonely melody.
Come near, that no more blinded by man's fate,
I find under the boughs of love and hate,
In all poor foolish things that live a day,
Eternal beauty wandering on her way.

Come near, come near, come near—Ah, leave me still
A little space for the rose-breath to fill!
Lest I no more hear common things that crave;
The weak worm hiding down in its small cave,
The field mouse running by me in the grass,
And heavy mortal hopes that toil and pass;
But seek alone to hear the strange things said
By God to the bright hearts of those long dead,
And learn to chaunt a tongue men do not know.
Come near; I would, before my time to go,
Sing of old Eire and the ancient ways:
Red Rose, proud Rose, sad Rose of all my days.

W. B. YEATS

DOWN BY THE SALLEY GARDENS

Down by the salley gardens my love and I did meet;
She passed the salley gardens with little snow-white feet.
She bid me take love easy, as the leaves grow on the tree;
But I, young and foolish, with her would not agree.

In a field by the river my love and I did stand,
And on my leaning shoulder she laid her snow-white hand.
She bid me take life easy, as the grass grows on the weirs;
But I was young and foolish, and now am full of tears.

W. B. YEATS

THE KINE OF MY FATHER

The kine of my father, they are straying from my keeping;
  The young goat's at mischief, but little can I do:
For all through the night did I hear the banshee keening;
  O youth of my loving, and is it well with you?

All through the night sat my mother with my sorrow;
  "Wisht, it is the storm, O one childeen of my heart!"
My hair with the wind, and my two hands clasped in anguish;
  Black head of my darling! too long are we apart.

Were your grave at my feet, I would think it half a blessing;
  I could herd then the cattle, and drive the goats away;
Many a Paternoster I would say for your safe keeping;
  I could sleep above your heart until the dawn of day.

I see you on the prairie, hot with thirst and faint with hunger;
  The head that I love lying low upon the sand.
The vultures shriek impatient, and the coyote dogs are howling,
  Till the blood is pulsing cold within your clenching hand.

I see you on the waters, so white, so still, forsaken,
  Your dear eyes unclosing beneath a foreign rain:
A plaything of the winds, you turn and drift unceasing;
  No grave for your resting; Oh, mine the bitter pain!

All through the night did I hear the banshee keening:
  Somewhere you are dying, and nothing can I do:
My hair with the wind, and my two hands clasped in anguish;
  Bitter is your trouble—and I am far from you.

DORA SIGERSON SHORTER

MAY EVE

There's a crying at my window, and a
    hand upon my door,
And a stir among the yarrow that's fading on
    the floor:
The voice cries at my window, the hand at my
    door beats on,
But if I heed and answer them, sure, hand and
    voice are gone.

You would not heed my calling once, and now
    why would I hear?
You would not hold my wistful hand, but let
    it fall, my dear:
You would not give me word or look, but went
    your silent way,
Oh, wirrasthrue, dumb mouth of you that had
    so much to say.

Be still, my dear: I heed, I hear, but cannot
    help you now,
The rose is dead that was so red, and snow's
    upon her bough.
Be still, be still a little while, for I shall surely
    come
And kiss the sorrow from your eyes, and from
    your kind lips dumb.

Be patient now, avourneen! you may not lift
    the latch:
Go hence: the wind is bitter cold that whistles
    through the thatch.
The wind is cold, and I am old, but you're
    young and fair to see,
And my heart turns to you night and day, my
    fair love leaving me!

NORA CHESSON

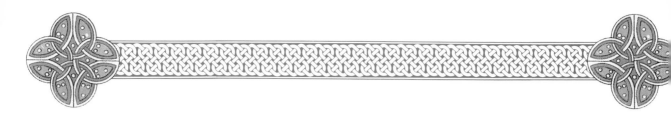

THE WAVES OF BREFFNY

The grand road from the mountain goes shining to the sea,
And there is traffic on it and many a horse and cart;
But the little roads of Cloonagh are dearer far to me
And the little roads of Cloonagh go rambling through my heart.

A great storm from the ocean goes shouting o'er the hill,
And there is glory in it, and terror on the wind;
But the haunted air of twilight is very strange and still,
And the little winds of twilight are dearer to my mind.

The great waves of the Atlantic sweep storming on their way,
Shining green and silver with the hidden herring shoal;
But the little waves of Breffny have drenched my heart in spray,
And the little waves of Breffny go stumbling through my soul.

EVA GORE-BOOTH

INISHAIL

I will go, and leave the streetways,
    And the world's wild, dinsome places,
With the hurrying, weary feetways,
    And the folks of frenzied faces;
    I will go through darkened spaces,
Morning glad, or starlight pale,
    Through the rivers and the passes,
    Till I find, among the grasses,
    Long sweet sleep among the grasses
Of the graves of Inishail.

Ah, ye daunt me, with your wonder,
    And your toils about you lying,
O ye cities, with your thunder,
    And your children in you, dying,
    And I weary, ever sighing,
For the whisper of the West,
    Where the glow and glamour meeting,
    And the waves on long shores beating,
    Are but echoes of the beating
Of the life's blood in my breast.

I will plait a roof of rashes
    For the low place of my sleeping,
Where the wistful water plashes,
    Crooning, croodling, laughing, weeping,
    And the winds from Cruachan sweeping
Join their gladness and their wail;
    Till the angels' glory blinds me,
    And the long sleep comes and finds me,
    In the tangled grasses finds me,
By the graves in Inishail.

AUTHOR UNKNOWN

BEG-INNISH

Bring Kateen-beug and Maurya Jude
    To dance in Beg-Innish,
And when the lads (they're in Dunquin)
    Have sold their crabs and fish,
Wave fawny shawls and call them in,
And call the little girls who spin,
And seven weavers from Dunquin,
    To dance in Beg-Innish.

I'll play you jigs, and Maurice Kean,
    Where nets are laid to dry,
I've silken strings would draw a dance
    From girls are lame or shy;
Four strings I've brought from Spain and France
To make your long men skip and prance,
Till stars look out to see the dance
    Where nets are laid to dry.

We'll have no priest or peeler in
    To dance in Beg-Innish;
But we'll have drink from M'riarty Jim
    Rowed round while gannets fish,
A keg with porter to the brim,
That every lad may have his whim,
Till we up sails with M'riarty Jim
    And sail from Beg-Innish.

JOHN MILLINGTON SYNGE

THE MOTHER

I do not grudge them; Lord, I do not grudge
My two strong sons that I have seen go out
To break their strength and die, they and a few,
In bloody protest for a glorious thing.
They shall be spoken of among their people,
The generations shall remember them,
And call them blessed;
But I will speak their names to my own heart
In the long nights;
The little names that were familiar once
Round my dead hearth.
Lord, thou art hard on mothers:
We suffer in their coming and their going;
And tho' I grudge them not, I weary, weary
Of the long sorrow—And yet I have my joy:
My sons were faithful and they fought.

PADRAIC PEARSE

TO MY DAUGHTER BETTY, THE GIFT OF GOD

In wiser days, my darling rosebud, blown
To beauty proud as was your mother's prime,
In that desired, delayed, incredible time,
You'll ask why I abandoned you, my own,
And the dear heart that was your baby throne,
To dice with death. And oh! they'll give you rhyme
And reason: some will call the thing sublime,
And some decry it in a knowing tone.
So here, while the mad guns curse overhead,
And tired men sigh with mud for couch and floor,
Know that we fools, now with the foolish dead,
Died not for flag, nor King, nor Emperor—
But for a dream, born in a herdman's shed,
And for the secret Scripture of the poor.

THOMAS M. KETTLE

A BROKEN SONG

"Where am I from?" From the green hills of Erin.
"Have I no song then?" My songs are all sung.
"What o' my love?" 'T is alone I am farin'.
Old grows my heart, an' my voice yet is young.

"If she was tall?" Like a king's own daughter.
"If she was fair?" Like a mornin' o' May.
When she'd come laughin' 'twas the runnin' wather,
When she'd come blushin' 'twas the break o' day.

"Where did she dwell?" Where one'st I had my dwellin'.
"Who loved her best?" There' no one now will know.
"Where is she gone?" Och, why would I be tellin'!
Where she is gone there I can never go.

MOIRA O'NEILL

SEA WRACK

The wrack was dark an' shiny where it floated in the sea,
There was no one in the brown boat but only him an' me;
Him to cut the sea wrack, me to mind the boat,
An' not a word between us the hours we were afloat.

    The wet wrack,

    The sea wrack,

    The wrack was strong to cut.

We laid it on the gray rocks to wither in the sun,
An' what should call my lad then, to sail from Cushendun?
With a low moon, a full tide, a swell upon the deep,
Him to sail the old boat, me to fall asleep.

    The dry wrack,

    The sea wrack,

    The wrack was dead so soon.

There' a fire low upon the rocks to burn the wrack to kelp,
There' a boat gone down upon the Moyle, an' sorra one to help!
Him beneath the salt sea, me upon the shore,
By sunlight or moonlight we'll lift the wrack no more.

    The dark wrack,

    The sea wrack,

    The wrack may drift ashore.

MOIRA O'NEILL

THE HERONS

As I was climbing Ardan Mór
From the shore of Sheelin lake,
I met the herons coming down
Before the water's wake.

And they were talking in their flight
Of dreamy ways the herons go
When all the hills are withered up
Nor any waters flow.

FRANCIS LEDWIDGE

A LITTLE BOY IN THE MORNING

He will not come, and still I wait.
He whistles at another gate
Where angels listen. Ah, I know
He will not come, yet if I go
How shall I know he did not pass
Barefooted in the flowery grass?

The moon leans on one silver horn
Above the silhouettes of morn,
And from their nest sills finches whistle
Or stooping pluck the downy thistle.
How is the morn so gay and fair
Without his whistling in its air?
The world is calling, I must go.
How shall I know he did not pass
Barefooted in the shining grass?

FRANCIS LEDWIDGE